November 2011   Gift   87787 $ 19.54

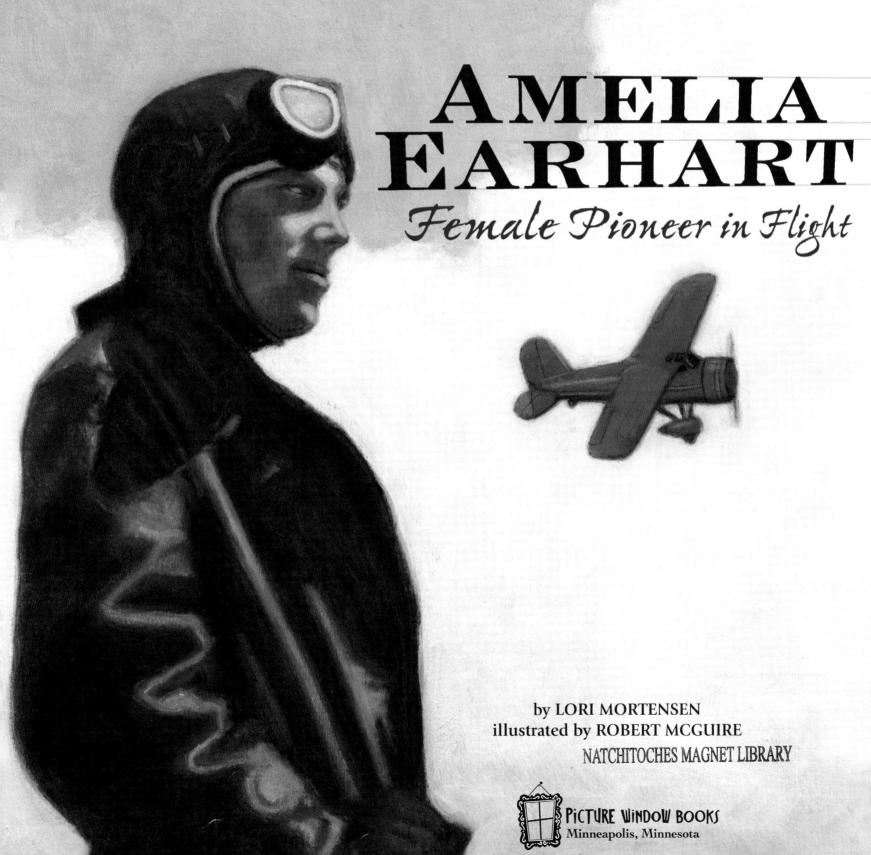

BIOGRAPHIES

AMELIA EARHART
Female Pioneer in Flight

by LORI MORTENSEN
illustrated by ROBERT MCGUIRE
NATCHITOCHES MAGNET LIBRARY

PICTURE WINDOW BOOKS
Minneapolis, Minnesota

Special thanks to our advisers for their expertise:

Sammie L. Morris, MLIS, Assistant Professor of Library Science
Head of Archives and Special Collections, Purdue University Libraries
West Lafayette, Indiana

Terry Flaherty, Ph.D., Professor of English
Minnesota State University, Mankato

Editors: Jill Kalz and Shelly Lyons
Designer: Nathan Gassman
Page Production: Michelle Biedscheid
Associate Managing Editor: Christianne Jones
The illustrations in this book were created with oils.
Photo Credit: Library of Congress, page 3

Picture Window Books
151 Good Counsel Drive
P.O. Box 669
Mankato, MN 56002-0669
877-845-8392
www.capstonepub.com

All books published by Picture Window Books
are manufactured with paper containing at least
10 percent post-consumer waste.

Library of Congress Cataloging-in-Publication Data
Mortensen, Lori, 1955-
Amelia Earhart : female pioneer in flight / by Lori Mortensen ; illustrated by
Robert McGuire.
p. cm.
ISBN-13: 978-1-4048-3728-7 (library binding)
ISBN-10: 1-4048-3728-0 (library binding)
1. Earhart, Amelia, 1897-1937—Juvenile literature. 2. Air pilots—United States—
Biography—Juvenile literature. 3. Women air pilots—United States—Biography—
Juvenile literature. I. McGuire, Robert, 1978- ill. II. Title.
TL540.E3M665 2008
629.13092—dc22
[B]   2007004294

Printed in the United States of America in North Mankato, Minnesota.
122010   006036R

Amelia Earhart was one of the most famous women in history. She flew airplanes when people believed a woman's only place was in the home. But Amelia didn't care what others thought. She followed her dream and flew all over the world. Amelia showed women they could follow their dreams, too.

This is the story of
Amelia Earhart.

4

Amelia Earhart was born in Atchison, Kansas, on July 24, 1897. Back then, girls were expected to wear dresses, talk softly, and sit quietly. But Amelia wore knee-length bloomers, climbed trees, and played baseball. She was a bold and daring girl.

When she was 7 years old, Amelia saw a roller coaster at a county fair. Her mother said it was too dangerous to ride.

When Amelia got home, she and her younger sister, Muriel, built their own roller coaster. Amelia was the first one to ride down the wooden track.

During Amelia's childhood, Amelia's family moved many times. Amelia went to many different schools. She worked hard in school and did well in math and science.

Other students thought highly of Amelia's strong mind, but she was not popular. The words beneath one of Amelia's yearbook pictures read, "Amelia Earhart—the girl in brown who walks alone."

In 1908, Amelia saw her first airplane at the Iowa State Fair. She said it looked like a mess of rusty wire and wood. It would be 10 more years before Amelia's love for planes would blossom.

Amelia graduated from high school in 1915. She later started college in Pennsylvania. But after Amelia traveled to Canada to visit her sister and saw soldiers who were wounded in World War I (1914–1918), school seemed unimportant. She left her studies and became a nurse's aide.

Then one day in 1918, Amelia saw an air show with a friend. Afterward, as a joke, a stunt pilot flew his airplane straight at them. Amelia's friend ran for safety. But not Amelia. She stood her ground and decided one day she would fly.

9

In 1920, Amelia moved to Los Angeles, California. She paid $10 for her first plane ride and soon took flying lessons. At first, Amelia was not a natural pilot. But she soon learned how to perform stunts and take care of an engine.

Amelia bought her first plane for her 24th birthday. She called it the *Canary* because of its bright yellow color.

One day in 1928, Hilton H. Railey called Amelia. He asked her if she would join two other pilots and be the first woman to ride in a plane across the Atlantic Ocean. Amelia said yes.

On June 17–18, 1928, Amelia rode in a plane called *Friendship* from Canada to Wales. The flight lasted 20 hours and 40 minutes. Newspaper headlines announced, "GIRL PILOT DARES THE ATLANTIC."

When Amelia returned to the United States, she was famous. Across the country, parades were held in her honor. But Amelia wasn't satisfied being just a passenger. Next time, she wanted to fly the plane herself.

Three years later, Amelia married George Putnam. Together, they planned Amelia's next adventure—to fly a plane across the Atlantic Ocean by herself.

Amelia took off in her Lockheed Vega on May 20, 1932. At first, the weather was clear. Then Amelia hit a storm. Winds shook her plane. Lightning flashed. Later, her engine caught fire. Still, Amelia kept flying. By early afternoon she reached land—a farmer's field in Ireland.

Amelia not only became the first woman to fly an airplane across the Atlantic Ocean, but she was also the first woman to do it solo. Before Amelia, only one other person had flown solo across the Atlantic Ocean. That person was Charles Lindbergh.

In 1936, Amelia planned the longest world flight ever. She would fly around the world at the equator, covering 29,000 miles (46,400 kilometers).

Amelia and her navigator took off in a Lockheed Electra from Miami, Florida, on June 1, 1937. Over the next month, they flew to Puerto Rico, South America, Africa, Asia, Australia, and New Guinea.

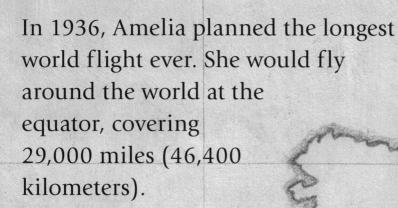

NORTH AMERICA

Miami, Florida

SOUTH AMERICA

From there, Amelia planned to fly across the Pacific Ocean to Howland, an island 2,556 miles (4,090 km) away. The island was so tiny that a coast guard ship waited nearby to guide Amelia by radio.

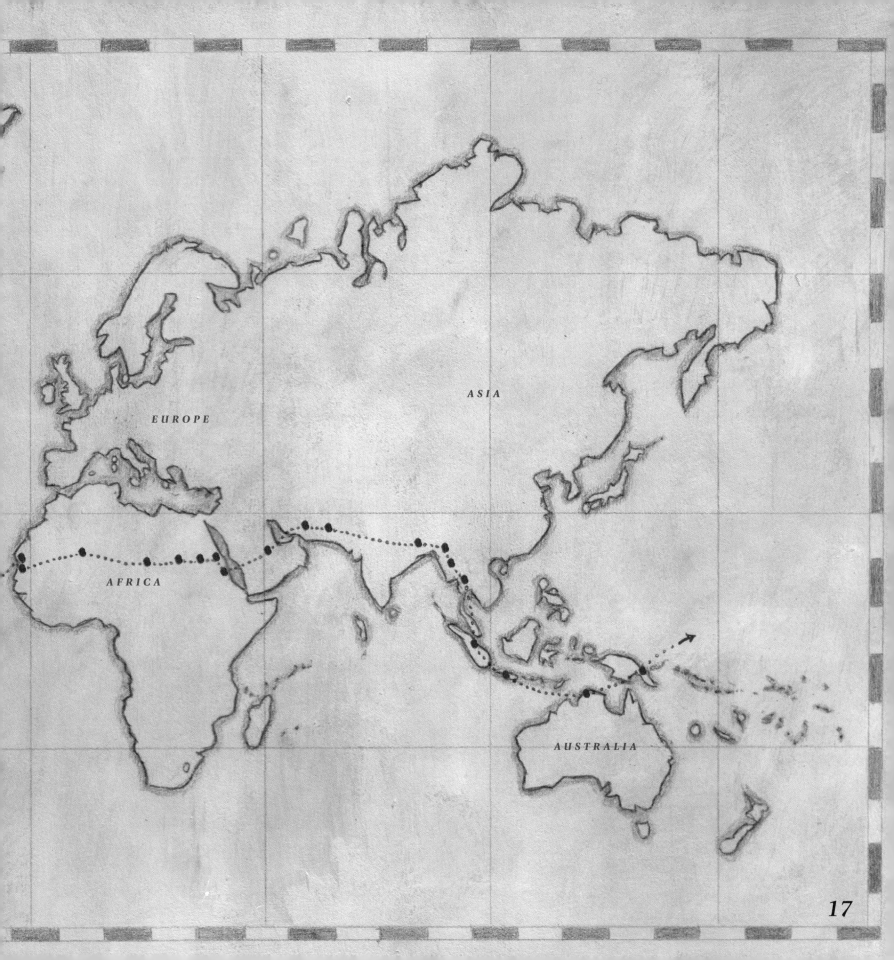

EUROPE

ASIA

AFRICA

AUSTRALIA

Amelia never reached Howland Island. After 14 hours, the radio crew finally heard her voice. But static was heavy, and they could not understand each other. They received her last radio message at 8:44 a.m. on July 2.

No traces of Amelia, her navigator, or her plane were ever found. She was just weeks shy of turning 40.

Today, Amelia's disappearance is still a mystery. But there is no mystery about her life. Amelia boldly followed her dreams and showed others they could follow their dreams, too.

The Life of Amelia Earhart

1897	Born in Atchison, Kansas, on July 24
1904	Built a roller coaster in her backyard
1915	Graduated from high school in Chicago
1917	Became a nurse's aide for the Red Cross
1918	Saw an air show and decided she wanted to fly
1920	Rode in an airplane for the first time
1921	Began taking flying lessons; bought her first airplane
1928	Became the first woman to fly across the Atlantic Ocean as a passenger
1931	Married George Palmer Putnam
1932	Became the first woman to pilot a plane across the Atlantic Ocean
1937	Began a flight around the world and disappeared near Howland Island

Did You Know?

~ One winter, young Amelia zoomed down a hill on a sled. Before she got to the bottom, a man with his horse and cart crossed her path. Instead of crashing, she shot safely between the horse's legs.

~ Amelia was also known as "Lady Lindy." The name was given to her because the first man to fly across the Atlantic Ocean was Charles Lindbergh. Amelia was the second person and the first woman to fly solo across the Atlantic Ocean.

~ Amelia set many flying records and earned many awards. She set a record by flying at an altitude of 14,000 feet (4,270 meters). Later, she became the first person to fly across the Pacific Ocean from Hawaii to California. She received a gold medal from the National Geographic Society. She was also the first woman to receive the U.S. Distinguished Flying Cross.

~ The U.S. government spent $4 million searching for Amelia. At the time, it was the most extensive air and sea search ever attempted.

Glossary

equator — an imaginary line around the middle of Earth; it divides the northern half and the southern half

Lockheed Electra — a huge, two-engine plane made by Lockheed Corporation; it was so big it could carry enough fuel to fly for 4,000 miles (6,400 kilometers) before refueling

Lockheed Vega — a rugged, single-engine plane made by Lockheed Corporation

navigator — a person or device that guides the course of an airplane

static — electrical charges in the air; the charges cause crackling noises in radio broadcasts

stunt — a daring act done for attention

To Learn More

At the Library

Ford, Carin T. *Amelia Earhart: Meet the Pilot.* Berkeley Heights, N.J.: Enslow Publishers, 2002.

Lakin, Patricia. *Amelia Earhart: More than a Flyer.* New York: Aladdin, 2003.

Mara, Wil. *Amelia Earhart.* New York: Children's Press, 2002.

Schaefer, Lola M. *Amelia Earhart.* Mankato, Minn.: Capstone Press, 2002.

On the Web

FactHound offers a safe, fun way to find Web sites related to this book. All of the sites on FactHound have been researched by our staff.

1. Visit *www.facthound.com*

2. Type in this special code: 1404837280

3. Click on the FETCH IT button.

Your trusty FactHound will fetch the best sites for you!

Index

air and sea search, 23
air show, 8, 22
airplane, 7, 8, 10, 11, 12, 13, 14, 15, 16, 19, 22
Atlantic Ocean, 12, 14, 15, 22, 23
birth, 5, 22
Earhart, Muriel, 5
family, 6, 8
flying lessons, 10, 22
flying records and awards, 23
Howland Island, 16, 19, 22
Iowa State Fair, 7
Lindbergh, Charles 15, 23
Lockheed Electra, 16
Lockheed Vega, 15
Los Angeles, 10
nurse's aide, 8, 22
Pacific Ocean, 16, 23
Putnam, George Palmer, 14, 22
Railey, Hilton H., 12
roller coaster, 5, 22
school, 6, 8, 22

Look for all of the books in the Biographies series:

Abraham Lincoln: *Lawyer, President, Emancipator*

Albert Einstein: *Scientist and Genius*

Amelia Earhart: *Female Pioneer in Flight*

Benjamin Franklin: *Writer, Inventor, Statesman*

Cesar Chavez: *Champion and Voice of Farmworkers*

Frederick Douglass: *Writer, Speaker, and Opponent of Slavery*

George Washington: *Farmer, Soldier, President*

George Washington Carver: *Teacher, Scientist, and Inventor*

Harriet Tubman: *Hero of the Underground Railroad*

Martha Washington: *First Lady of the United States*

Martin Luther King Jr.: *Preacher, Freedom Fighter, Peacemaker*

Pocahontas: *Peacemaker and Friend to the Colonists*

Sally Ride: *Astronaut, Scientist, Teacher*

Sojourner Truth: *Preacher for Freedom and Equality*

Susan B. Anthony: *Fighter for Freedom and Equality*

Thomas Edison: *Inventor, Scientist, and Genius*